CAMBRIDGE PRIMARY
Science

Challenge

5

Fiona Baxter and Liz Dilley

CAMBRIDGE
UNIVERSITY PRESS

University Printing House, Cambridge CB2 8BS, United Kingdom

Cambridge University Press is part of the University of Cambridge.

It furthers the University's mission by disseminating knowledge in the pursuit of education, learning and research at the highest international levels of excellence.

Information on this title: education.cambridge.org

© Cambridge University Press 2016

First published 2016

Produced for Cambridge University Press by
White-Thomson Publishing
www.wtpub.co.uk

Editor: Sonya Newland
Designer: Tracey Camden

Printed in Poland by Opolgraf

A catalogue record for this publication is available from the British Library

ISBN 978-1-316-61120-3 Paperback

Additional resources for this publication at www.cambridge.org/

....

Contents

Introduction

This series of primary science activity books complements *Cambridge Primary Science* and progresses, through practice, learner confidence and depth of knowledge in the skills of scientific enquiry (SE) and key scientific vocabulary and concepts. These activity books will:

- enhance and extend learners' scientific knowledge and facts
- promote scientific enquiry skills and learning in order to think like a scientist
- advance each learner's knowledge and use of scientific vocabulary and concepts in their correct context.

The *Challenge* activity books extend learners' understanding of the main curriculum, providing an opportunity to increase the depth of their knowledge and scientific enquiry skills from a key selection of topics. This workbook is offered as extension to the main curriculum and therefore it does not cover all the curriculum framework content for this stage.

How to use the activity books

These activity books have been designed for use by individual learners, either in the classroom or at home. As teachers and as parents, you can decide how and when they are used by your learner to best improve their progress. The *Challenge* activity books target specific topics (lessons) from Grades 1–6 from all the units covered in *Cambridge Primary Science*. This targeted approach has been carefully designed to consolidate topics where help is most needed.

How to use the units

Unit introduction

Each unit starts with an introduction for you as the teacher or parent. It clearly sets out which topics are covered in the unit and the learning objectives of the activities in each section. This is where you can work with learners to select all, most or just one of the sections according to individual needs.

The introduction also provides advice and tips on how best to support the learner in the skills of scientific enquiry and in the practice of key scientific vocabulary.

Sections

Each section matches a corresponding lesson in the main series. Sections contain write-in activities that are supported by:

- Key words – key vocabulary for the topic, also highlighted in bold in the sections
- Key facts – a short fact to support the activities where relevant
- Look and learn – where needed, activities are supported with scientific exemplars for extra support of how to treat a concept or scientific method
- Remember – tips for the learner to steer them in the right direction.

How to approach the write-in activities

Teachers and parents are advised to provide students with a blank A5 notebook at the start of each grade for learners to use alongside these activity books. Most activities will provide enough space for the answers required. However, some learner responses – especially to enquiry-type questions – may require more space for notes. Keeping notes and plans models how scientists work and encourages learners to explore and record their thinking, leaving the activity books for the final, more focused answers.

Think about it questions

Each unit also contains some questions for discussion at home with parents, or at school. Although learners will record the outcomes of their discussions in the activity book, these questions are intended to encourage the students to think more deeply.

Self-assessment

Each section in the unit ends with a self-assessment opportunity for learners: empty circles with short learning statements. Teachers or parents can ask learners to complete the circles in a number of ways, depending on their age and preference, e.g. with faces, traffic light colours or numbers. The completed self-assessments provide teachers with a clearer understanding of how best to progress and support individual learners.

Glossary of key words and concepts

At the end of each activity book there is a glossary of key scientific words and concepts arranged by unit. Learners are regularly reminded to practise saying these words out loud and in sentences to improve communication skills in scientific literacy.

1 Investigating plant growth

The unit challenge

The activities in this Challenge unit will extend learners' knowledge of the following topics from the Learner's Book and Activity Book:

Topic	In this topic, learners will:
1.3 Investigating germination	complete a report on an investigation into germination
1.4 What do plants need to grow?	make a cutting, then measure and draw a graph of its growth
1.5 Plants and light	decide which type of graph to draw and make drawings of leaves

Help your learner

In this unit, learners will practise presenting results in a line graph (Sections 1.4 and 1.5), recognising the need for repeated measurements, making a prediction and using knowledge and understanding to plan how to carry out a fair test (Section 1.3). They will also practise measuring length (Section 1.4). To help them:

1 Remind learners that we use a line graph to show how something changes with time. Line graphs always have numbers on both axes. Learners should plot the data points first and then join them neatly with pencil. Do not use a ruler, as the graphs do not always have straight lines.

TEACHING TIP

Remind learners that when they are measuring increasing length, they should measure from the same point each time.

factors, seeds, germinate, evidence

Complete a report about germination

Kumei investigated one of the **factors** that **seeds** need to **germinate**. She took two plant pots and put three radish seeds in each pot. Kumei observed how long it took for the first seed to germinate in each pot. She then repeated her investigation. These are her results:

Place where plants kept	Time for first seed to germinate (days)	
	Test 1	Test 2
Pot A: windowsill	3	2
Pot B: cupboard	2	3

1 Fill in the spaces on Kumei's report.

Aim: I am going to investigate if seeds need _____ to germinate.

Factors I will keep the same are: _____

_____

_____

I will change _____

I will measure _____

My prediction is that the seeds in Pot A/Pot B/both pots will germinate faster/slower/ at the same rate.

My conclusion is that seeds _____ for germination.

2 Why do you think Kumei planted three seeds in each pot?

_____

_____

3 Does Kumei have enough **evidence** to be sure her conclusion is correct? Explain why or why not.

_____

_____

4 What can Kumei do to find out if her conclusion is only true of radish seeds?

_____

_____

_____

5 **Think about it!**

Some seeds need smoke to germinate. Find out which plants have seeds that only germinate after a fire.

> **Remember:**
>
> Repeating a test or investigation means you can check if your first set of results was correct and make sure there were no mistakes in measuring or recording the results.

_____

_____

CHECK YOUR LEARNING

◯ I can plan a fair test.

◯ I can explain why we need to repeat measurements in an investigation.

◯ I can decide if I have enough evidence to draw a conclusion.

Grow a plant from a cutting

> **Resources**
> You will need a plant with a soft stem, such as a geranium, begonia, busy Lizzie (*impatiens*), basil, mint or cilantro (also called coriander or dhania). You will also need scissors, an empty jar, water, a waterproof permanent marker and a ruler.

Follow these steps to grow a new plant from a cutting.

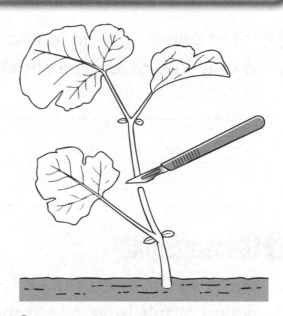

- Cut a piece off a stem as shown in the drawing.

- Pull off the lower leaves on the stem cutting, but leave one or two leaves at the top.

- Put the stem cutting in a jar of water.

- Leave the jar for a few days, then see the cutting grow.

1 **Where is a good place to leave the jar? Think about the factors plants need for growth.**

⚠ Always take care when using a scalpel. Get an adult to help you.

_____

2 **Which part of the new plant do you think will grow first?**

> **KEY FACT**
> Plants need water, warmth, light and air to grow.

_____

3 Measure the growth of the new plant every four days for 12 days. Record your measurements in the table.

Day	Length (mm)
1	0
4	
8	
12	

Remember:

Measure from the same point each time. Mark that point on the plant with the marker pen.

4 Draw a graph of the plant's growth. Think about the kind of graph you will draw.

CHECK YOUR LEARNING

◯ I know how to grow a new plant from a cutting.

◯ I can measure length.

◯ I can identify the factors that plants need for growth.

◯ I can draw a line graph.

Investigate plant growth

Carla and Maria observed the growth of plants A and B once a week for four weeks.

Plant A   Plant B

They counted the number of leaves on each plant. These are their results:

Week	Number of leaves	
	Plant A	Plant B
1	6	6
2	10	8
3	12	10
4	15	10

1 Draw a graph of the results.

2 Which plant grew better? What evidence shows this?

_____

_____

3 Make drawings of how you think a leaf on each plant looked after four weeks.

<table>
<tr><td></td><td></td></tr>
</table>

Plant A   Plant B

4 Which factor that affects plant growth caused these results?

_____

_____

CHECK YOUR LEARNING

○ I can choose the correct type of graph to draw.

○ I can explain what the evidence from an investigation shows.

○ I can make drawings to show how light affects the leaves of plants.

KEY FACT

A substance called chlorophyll gives plants their green colour. Plants need light to make chlorophyll. If they do not get enough light, their leaves turn pale and yellow.

2 The life cycle of flowering plants

The unit challenge

The activities in this Challenge unit will extend learners' knowledge of the following topics from the Learner's Book and Activity Book:

Topic	In this topic, learners will:
2.1 Why plants have flowers	see Skills Builder, Section 2.1
2.2 How seeds are spread	identify ways animals disperse seeds
2.3 Other ways seeds are spread	analyse the results of an investigation and identify a pattern in the results
2.4 The parts of a flower	label a diagram of a flower and suggest reasons for the flower's structure
2.5 Pollination	See Skills Builder, Section 2.5
2.6 Investigating pollination	read and answer questions about the cannonball tree
2.7 Plant life cycles	choose correct answers to questions about plant life cycles

Help your learner

In this unit, learners will practise recognising patterns in data and suggesting explanations for them, thinking about the need for repeated measurements and identifying factors that need to be taken into account in a fair test (Section 2.3). To help them:

1 Remind learners that identifying patterns in results is not done by guessing. They must use their observation skills and scientific knowledge and understanding.

2 Talk about why scientists present data in graphs. We can think of a graph as a 'picture' of data. Graphs are useful because they can reveal patterns and can be used to make predictions.

TEACHING TIP

Try to make this unit as practical as possible by observing seeds, flowers and pollinators if you can.

2.2 How seeds are spread

dispersed

LOOK AND LEARN

Seeds can be spread through animal droppings, by getting caught on fur then falling off in a different place or by being buried by animals for food.

Identify ways that animals disperse seeds

Look at the pictures of the three seeds.

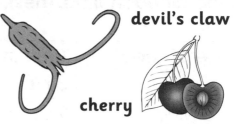

devil's claw

cherry

sunflower

1 Fill in the table to identify the way the seed or fruit is **dispersed**.

Seed	An animal that disperses the seed	Way the seed is dispersed

2 Explain why the cherry is suited to its way of dispersal.

_____

_____

3 Explain why the devil's claw seed is suited to its way of dispersal.

_____

_____

CHECK YOUR LEARNING

◯ I can explain the way seeds are dispersed by animals.

◯ I can explain why some seeds are suited to their way of dispersal.

Analyse the results of an experiment with seeds

Ahmed and Yaseen collected three different **wind-dispersed** seeds. They dropped each seed three times and measured how long it stayed in the air each time. These are their results:

Type of seed	Time in the air 1	Time in the air 2	Time in the air 3	Average time in the air
one-winged sycamore seed	9 seconds	10 seconds	11 seconds	
dandelion parachute	20 seconds	22 seconds	24 seconds	
two-winged helicopter tree seed	15 seconds	13 seconds	17 seconds	

Ahmed and Yaseen also held the seeds in front of a fan then let them go. They measured the distance each seed travelled three times. These are their results:

Type of seed	Distance travelled 1	Distance travelled 2	Distance travelled 3	Average distance travelled
one-winged sycamore seed	1.8 m	2.0 m	2.2 m	
dandelion parachute seed	4.5 m	4.1 m	4.3 m	
two-winged helicopter tree seed	2.0 m	2.4 m	2.2 m	

1 **a** Work out the **average** time each seed stayed in the air. Write the times in the first table.

b Work out the average distance each seed travelled. Write the distances in the second table.

2 Why did Ahmed and Yaseen repeat their measurements?

_____

3 Identify the pattern shown in the results. Suggest a reason for the pattern.

_____

_____

_____

4 **a** Identify two factors that might affect the length of time that the seeds stayed in the air.

_____

_____

b Identify two factors that might affect the distance travelled by the seeds.

_____

_____

_____

5 What did Ahmed and Yaseen do to make this a fair test?

_____

_____

_____

CHECK YOUR LEARNING

◯ I can calculate averages.

◯ I can identify factors that affect how long a seed stays in the air and how far it travels.

◯ I can identify factors needed to make a fair test.

Remember:

In a fair test, the only factor that should change is the factor you are measuring or observing.

2.4 The parts of a flower

Label the parts of a flower

LOOK AND LEARN

Not all flowers have all four main flower parts. Some flowers have either male or female parts, but not both. Other flowers may have **sepals** and no petals, or petals and no sepals.

Look at the drawing of a flower.

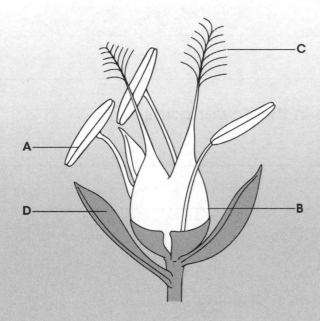

1 Write labels on the drawing for parts A, B, C and D.

2 Which part of the flower is missing?

_____

3 What colour would you expect the following parts to be? Explain your answers.

a Part A

_____

_____

_____

b Part D

_____

_____

_____

4 Describe any pattern you can see in the flower parts.

_____

_____

CHECK YOUR LEARNING

◯ I can identify the parts of a flower on a drawing.

◯ I can suggest reasons for the colour and shape of different parts of a flower.

2.6 Investigating pollination

Find out about the cannonball tree

Read about the cannonball tree, then answer the questions.

The cannonball tree grows in different countries around the world, such as India, Sri Lanka in Asia, and Guyana and Venezuela in South America. It is related to the Brazil nut tree. The cannonball tree grows for up to ten years before it starts to flower and form fruit.

The flowers grow on long branches that hang from the tree trunk. One tree can have as many as 1000 flowers on it. The flowers are big, waxy, dark pink and gold in colour with a strong, sweet scent. Fruit bats visit the trees at night when they are flowering to eat **pollen**. Bees also visit the flowers to find pollen.

The fruits of the cannonball tree are large, round and heavy. When they fall to the ground, they often make loud and explosive noises as they break open. The inside of the fruit has a bad smell – people say it smells like vomit! Animals are attracted by the smell and like to eat the fruit.

1 Why do you think the cannonball tree is called this?

_____

_____

2 a Name two ways that the flowers attract insects.

_____

_____

b Describe how the flowers attract bats. Why do you think this is?

_____

_____

_____

c What do the bats and insects do to help the cannonball tree's life cycle?

_____

_____

3 a In what way does the fruit help to disperse the seeds?

_____

_____

_____

b Explain how animals disperse the seeds of the cannonball tree.

_____

_____

c How many fruits can the cannonball tree form? Explain your answer.

_____

_____

_____

_____

4 Think about it!

Where did the cannonball tree originate? Does it grow in your country?

_____

_____

_____

CHECK YOUR LEARNING

◯ I can identify ways that flowers attract pollinators.

◯ I can explain the way that fruits and animals help seed dispersal.

◯ I can explain how fruits form.

life cycle, pollination, germination, fertilisation, embryo, pollinators

Describe the life cycle of plants

Look at the questions about the **life cycle** of plants. Circle the letter for the correct answer to each question.

Remember:

Practise saying these words out loud. Try to use them when talking about the topic.

1 The correct order of stages in a plant's life cycle is …

a pollination → germination → fertilisation → growth → seed dispersal → seed production

b germination → pollination → growth → seed dispersal → fertilisation → seed production

c germination → growth → pollination → fertilisation → seed production → seed dispersal

d seed dispersal → growth → germination → fertilisation → pollination → seed production.

2 The plant gets flowers just …

a before fertilisation

b before pollination

c after pollination

d after fertilisation.

3 Fertilisation take place when ...

   a the pollen lands on the stigma

   b the **embryo** starts growing

   c the pollen joins with the egg in the ovary

   d the ovary forms the fruit.

4 Which statement about flowers is *not* true?

   a Flowers form seeds.

   b Flowers form fruit.

   c Flowers attract **pollinators**.

   d Flowers release seeds.

5 After fertilisation ...

   a seeds form

   b the fruit releases seeds

   c the plant dies

   d the flower grows a stalk.

CHECK YOUR LEARNING

I can explain the stages in the life cycle of a plant.

3 States of matter

The unit challenge

The activities in this Challenge unit will extend learners' knowledge of the following topics from the Learner's Book and Activity Book:

Topic	In this topic, learners will:
3.1 Evaporation	see Skills Builder, Section 3.1
3.2 Why evaporation is useful	see Skills Builder, Section 3.2
3.3 Investigating evaporation	draw a line graph of results and make a prediction
3.4 Investigating evaporation from a solution	explain how to recover the solute from a solution
3.5 Condensation	see Skills Builder, Section 3.5
3.6 The water cycle	see Skills Builder, Section 3.6
3.7 Boiling	read information from a graph and compare evaporation and boiling
3.8 Melting	draw a bar chart and look for a pattern in data
3.9 Measuring temperature	see Skills Builder, Section 3.9

Help your learner

In this unit, learners will practise making predictions based on scientific knowledge and understanding (Section 3.3) and presenting results in line graphs and bar charts (Sections 3.3 and 3.8). They will also practise recognising patterns in data and suggesting explanations for them and decide whether there is enough data to draw a conclusion (Section 3.8). To help them:

1 Remind learners that we use line graphs for presenting data that changes continuously over time.

TEACHING TIP

Evaporation, condensation, melting and boiling happen all around us. Point out examples in everyday life to learners.

Experiment with evaporation

Akia and Dembe investigated **evaporation** of water. They placed two containers of water on the windowsill. These are their results:

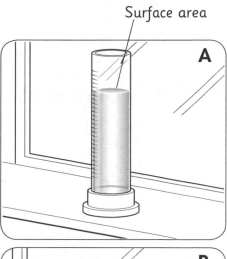

Surface area

A

Day	Volume of water in container (ml)	
	Container A	**Container B**
1	250	250
2	230	200
3	210	160
4	180	120
5	150	80
6		
7		

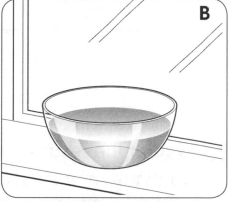

B

1 Draw a graph of the results for each container of water. Think about the type of graph you should draw.

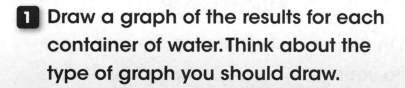

2 **a** In which container did most evaporation take place?
What tells you this?

_____

_____

b Which **factor** affected the amount of water that evaporated?

_____

c Explain why this factor affects evaporation.

_____

_____

_____

_____

3 Predict the results if Akia and Dembe continue their investigation for another two days. Fill in your prediction in the table and add the new points to your graph in another colour.

CHECK YOUR LEARNING

◯ I can draw a graph of results.

◯ I can use scientific knowledge and understanding to make a prediction.

KEY FACT

Evaporation can take place at any temperature. It does not need additional heat energy to happen, although heat and other factors – such as wind – will speed up the process.

solute, solvent, solution

Making solutions

Alicia poured hot water into a glass. She added a teaspoon of coffee powder. She stirred the water.

1 **a** Draw the glass of water and coffee before Alicia stirred it.

b Draw the glass of water and coffee after Alicia stirred it.

c Write the labels **solute**, **solvent** and **solution** on your drawings.

A
Before Alicia stirred

B
After Alicia stirred

2 What happened to the coffee powder when Alicia stirred the water?

_____

_____

_____

_____

3 What can Alicia do to get the coffee powder back again?

_____

_____

_____

LOOK AND LEARN

Try this activity for yourself. Ask an adult to help you make a solution of coffee powder and hot water in a glass. Always be careful when using hot water. You can also use powdered cooldrink and water. Observe the changes as the solute dissolves. Use the key words for the activity to talk about what is happening in the glass. Now use your answer to Question 3 to get the coffee or cooldrink powder back again.

CHECK YOUR LEARNING

◯ I can show what solution is in a drawing.

◯ I can explain what happens to the solute in a solution.

◯ I can explain how to use evaporation get the solute back from a solution.

3.7 Boiling

Compare temperatures at which liquids boil

The graph shows the **temperature** at which some different liquids **boil**.

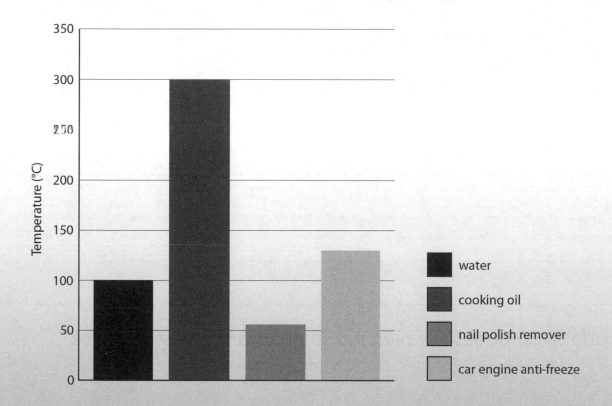

1 **What do we call the temperature at which a liquid boils?**

_____

2 **a** Which liquid boils at the highest temperature?

_____

b Which liquid boils at the lowest temperature?

_____

c At what temperature does car engine anti-freeze boil?

_____

3 **a** Describe the change of state that happens when a liquid boils.

_____

_____

_____

_____

b Name another process in which the same change of state takes place.

_____

KEY FACT

Water turns into a gas called water vapour when it is heated to a high enough temperature. We cannot see water vapour. The steam we see coming out of a kettle is water vapour that has condensed.

c   Complete the table to compare the two processes.

	Name of process: _____	Name of process: _____
Is the process fast or slow?		
Do bubbles form?		
At what temperature does it take place?		
Does it happen at the surface or throughout the liquid?		
Where does the energy needed for the process come from?		

4 Think about it!

Why is working with boiling oil more dangerous than working with boiling water?

_____

_____

CHECK YOUR LEARNING

◯   I can read information from a graph.

◯   I can describe the change of state when a liquid boils.

◯   I can name a process that has the same change of state as boiling and compare the two processes.

Compare the melting points of solids

Different solids **melt** at different temperatures. The table shows the
melting points of some solids.

Solid	Melting point (°C)
ice lolly	1
butter	35
lard (animal fat)	30
beeswax	62
margarine	36

1 Draw a graph of the data in the table. Think about the type of graph
you should draw.

2 a Which solid has the highest melting point?

_____

b Which solid has the lowest melting point?

_____

3 a What pattern do you notice in the data?

_____

b Is there enough data for you to reach a conclusion about the pattern you observed? Explain your answer.

_____

_____

_____

4 Why should people who live in very warm places keep butter and margarine in the fridge?

_____

_____

_____

CHECK YOUR LEARNING

◯ I can choose a suitable type of graph to draw and show results on it.

◯ I can find a pattern in data.

◯ I can decide if there is enough data to form a conclusion.

4 The way we see things

The unit challenge

The activities in this Challenge unit will extend learners' knowledge of the following topics in the Learner's Book and Activity Book:

Topic	In this topic, learners will:
4.1 Light travels from a source	know that light travels from a source and reflects off objects into our eyes
4.2 Mirrors	discover that mirrors reflect light well
4.3 Seeing behind you	see Skills Builder, Section 4.3
4.4 Which surfaces reflect light best?	See Skills Builder, Section 4.4
4.5 Light changes direction	show how light reflects off surfaces

Help your learner

In this unit, learners will practise making relevant observations (Sections 4.1 and 4.2) and making predictions of what will happen based on their scientific knowledge (Section 4.5). To help them:

1 Using Section 4.2 as a starting point, encourage learners to experiment with mirrors to ensure they have understood all the necessary concepts for this topic.

2 Ask learners to identify light sources at home and to explain how they are able to see things.

TEACHING TIP

Have some small mirrors available to help learners do the activities. Make sure the mirrors have bound edges otherwise learners could cut themselves.

4.1 Light travels from a source

Explain how we see objects

Sergio and Carlos are camping in the mountains with their father. It is evening and they have lit a fire to cook their supper.

KEY FACT

A **light source** can be natural, such as the Sun, or artificial, such as an electric lamp.

1 Name two sources of light in the picture.

_____

2 Carlos has gone to collect wood for the fire.

a Identify the **object** and the light source.

_____

b On the picture, draw lines with arrows to show how Carlos sees the wood.

3 Sergio and his father are sitting on opposite sides of the fire.

a Which light source allows Sergio to see his father?

_____

b On the picture, draw lines with arrows to show how Sergio sees his father.

4 Think about it!

If there was no Moon and no fire, what other light source could the campers use?

_____

CHECK YOUR LEARNING

◯ I know that light travels from a source and reflects off objects into my eyes.

◯ I can name different light sources.

Use mirrors to see in front of and behind you

Resources
You will need a friend, a sticky label, a marker pen, a small hand-held **mirror** and a large mirror on the wall. There must be an overhead light in the room.

Ask your friend to draw a picture on the sticky label with the marker pen and stick it on your back. They should not show you what it is.

1 If you stand facing the large mirror, what do you see in it?

_____

Use your two mirrors to see what the picture is on your back. Stand in different positions in front of or with your back to the mirror on the wall. Hold the small mirror in different positions until you can see the picture.

2 a Did you have to stand facing the mirror on the wall or with your back to the mirror on the wall?

_____

b Did you hold the small mirror in front of you, or in front and to one side of you?

_____

Remember:

Mirrors are smooth, shiny **surfaces** that **reflect** light well.

3 Draw a picture of how you saw the picture on your back. Draw four lines with arrows to **depict** the four stages of how the light travels from the light source to the sticker, and reflects off the mirrors and into your eyes.

CHECK YOUR LEARNING

◯ I can show how light travels from a source and reflects off objects into my eyes.

◯ I know that mirrors can help me to see behind me.

4.5 Light changes direction

Show how light is reflected

1 Look at the diagram showing light reflecting off a mirror.

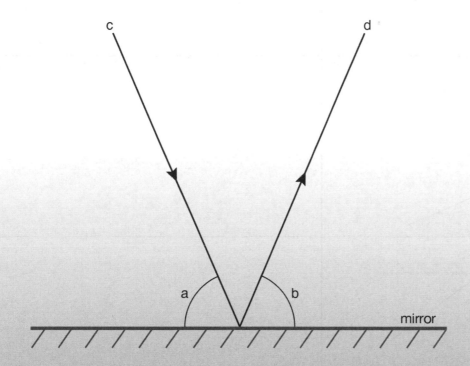

a What are the **beams** of light (c and d) called?

_____

b Which line represents the reflected light – c or d?

_____

c Are **angles** a and b the same or different?

_____

2 Look at the diagrams of light reflecting off another surface.

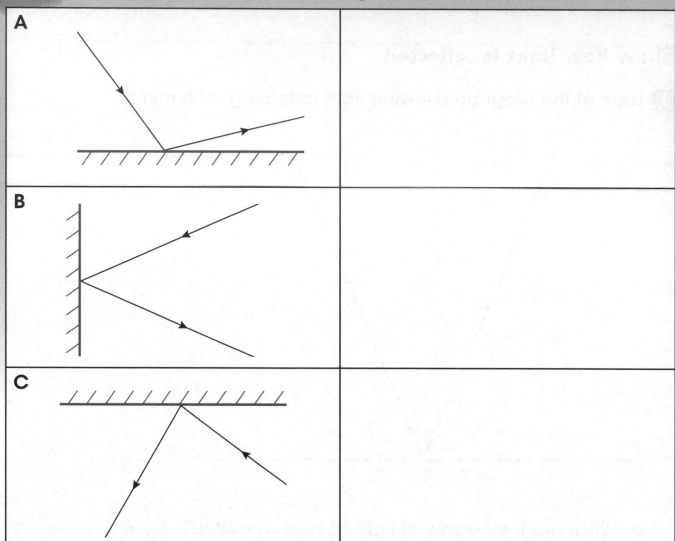

a Which diagram is correct – A, B or C?

_____

b Re-draw the diagrams that are incorrect in the spaces.

CHECK YOUR LEARNING

◯ I can show on diagrams how light reflects off surfaces.

◯ I know that a **ray** of light arrives at a mirror and reflects off it at the same angle.

5 Shadows

The activities in this Challenge unit will extend learners' knowledge of the following topics in the Learner's Book and Activity Book:

Topic	In this topic, learners will:
5.1 Light travels in straight lines	show that light travels in straight lines and shadows form when light is blocked by a solid object
5.2 Which materials let light through?	see Skills Builder, Section 5.2
5.3 Silhouettes and shadow puppets	see Skills Builder, Section 5.3
5.4 What affects the size of a shadow?	see Skills Builder, Section 5.4
5.5 Investigating shadow lengths	discover that shadows change in length throughout the day
5.6 Measuring light intensity	do an experiment to see how distance affects light intensity
5.7 How scientists measured and understood light	read about and compare how scientists measured the speed of light

Help your learner

In this unit, learners will practise making predictions and suggesting how to test them, using observations to test predictions and collecting sufficient evidence to test an idea (Sections 5.1 and 5.6). They will also practise interpreting data and thinking about whether it is sufficient to draw conclusions (Section 5.6) and presenting results in a line graph (Section 5.5). To help them:

1 Throughout the activities, keep asking learners what they *think* will happen at each stage to help them with making predictions.

2 Assist in choosing a scale for learners' line graphs in Section 5.5 if they are unsure.

evidence

Investigate the way light travels

Mira has a torch and a piece of plastic pipe that can be bent into shapes.

LOOK AND LEARN

When light is stopped or blocked by some kind of solid object, it cannot shine through the object.

1 Show in a drawing how Mira could provide **evidence** that light travels in straight lines.

2 Show in a drawing how Mira could provide evidence that light cannot turn corners.

CHECK YOUR LEARNING

I can demonstrate how light travels by collecting and analysing evidence.

5.5 Investigating shadow lengths

Observe how shadows change at different times of day

Viola, Sophie and Shruti like to sit on a bench under a small palm tree during school breaks. During morning break the bench is in full sun. At midday, the only shade is right below the palm tree. During the afternoon break at 15:00, the **shadow** of the palm tree is longer and it is nice and cool there. After school, at 16:30, the shadow is even longer.

1 a In the morning, is the Sun in front of the bench or behind the palm tree?

_____

b Where will the shadow be at this time?

_____

2 Why is there only shade immediately below the palm tree at midday?

_____

3 Why is the shadow longer at 15:00 and even longer at 16:30?

_____

_____

The girls decided to measure the length of the shadow cast by the palm tree at different times of day. Here are their results:

Time in hours	10:00	12:00	14:00	16:00
Length of shadow	100 cm	20 cm	110 cm	210 cm

Remember:

The size of a shadow is affected by the position of the object blocking the light source.

4 Draw a line graph to show these results.

CHECK YOUR LEARNING

◯ I can interpret data and reach conclusions about shadow lengths.

◯ I can draw a line graph.

Find out how distance affects light intensity

LOOK AND LEARN

Light intensity is a measure of the amount of light in an area. Brighter light means a higher light intensity. The more the light spreads out, the dimmer it becomes and the lower the light intensity.

Resources

You will need a small torch with new batteries in, a sheet of graph paper or squared paper, a measuring tape, a chair or stool and some sticky tape.

1 **Follow these steps:**

- Fix the torch to the seat of the chair or stool with tape.

- Tape the sheet of graph paper on the wall, directly opposite the torch.

- Measure 25 cm away from the wall. Place the torch on the chair at this point.

- Turn on the torch and shine it at the centre of the graph paper on the wall.

- Turn off the lights in the room.

- Measure the area the light covers by counting the squares that are lit up on the graph paper.

- Record the number of lit up squares in the table.

Distance of torch from wall	Number of squares lit up
25 cm	
50 cm	
75 cm	
1 m	

2 Predict whether more squares or fewer squares on the paper will be lit up if you move the torch further from the wall.

_____

3 Move the light source further away from the wall in 25 cm stages until you are 1 m from the wall. Count the number of squares that are lit up at each stage. Complete the table. Was your prediction correct?

4 Does a large number of lit-up squares show high or low light intensity?

_____

5 Circle the correct word in this sentence to write a **conclusion** about how distance affects light intensity:

The greater / smaller the distance, the lower the light intensity.

CHECK YOUR LEARNING

◯ I know that light intensity can be measured.

◯ I can make predictions and demonstrate that distance affects light intensity.

Measuring the speed of light

Read about the scientists who tried to measure the speed of light, then answer the questions.

Louis Fizeau

In 1849, the French physicist Louis Fizeau used a rapidly **rotating** toothed wheel with more than 100 teeth. He shone a **beam** of light between the teeth of the wheel. A mirror more than 8 km away reflected the beam back through the same gap. The wheel rotated at hundreds of times a second, so a fraction of a second was easy to measure. By varying the speed of the wheel, he worked out when the wheel was spinning too fast for the light to pass through the gap to the mirror then back through the same gap. He knew how far the light travelled and he measured the time it took with a stopwatch. By dividing the distance by the time, he got the speed of light. Fizeau measured the speed of light to be 313,300 km/s.

1 List the equipment that Fizeau used to measure the speed of light.

_____

_____

_____

2 What did Fizeau use to measure time?

_____

Leon Foucault

In 1862, another French physicist, Leon Foucault, used a similar method. He shone a light at a rotating mirror, then it bounced back to a fixed mirror, then back to the first rotating mirror. Because the first mirror was rotating, the light from it finally reflected back at an angle slightly different from the angle at which it hit the mirror the first time. By measuring this angle, he was able to measure the speed of the light. Foucault continually increased the accuracy of this method over the years. His final measurement in 1862 was that light travelled at 299,796 km/s.

3 List the equipment that Foucault used to measure the speed of light.

_____

_____

4 What did Foucault measure in order to calculate the speed of light?

_____

_____

5 The figure we use today for the speed of light using the most up-to-date digital equipment is 299,792.458 km/s.

Complete the table to show how the measurement of the speed of light has changed over time.

Date	Scientist	Speed of light
	Louis Fizeau	
		299,796 km/s
Today		

6 Think about it!

In 1638, the Italian scientist Galileo tried to work out the speed of light. What equipment did he use? What were his results? You will need to do some research to find out.

_____

_____

_____

_____

_____

_____

CHECK YOUR LEARNING

◯ I know that scientists base their ideas on observations and evidence from experiments.

◯ I know that ways of measuring the speed of light have changed over the last few hundred years.

6 Earth's movements

The activities in this Skills Builder unit give learners further practice in the following topics in the Learner's Book and Activity Book:

Topic	In this topic, learners will:
6.1 The Sun, the Earth and the Moon	see Skills Builder, Section 6.1
6.2 Does the Sun move?	see Skills Builder, Section 6.2
6.3 The Earth rotates on its axis	see Skills Builder, Section 6.3
6.4 Sunrise and sunset	analyse sunrise and sunset times
6.5 The Earth revolves around the Sun	understand the effect that revolution has on seasons
6.6 Exploring the solar system	find out about different comet discoveries
6.7 Exploring the stars	understand how astronomers have collected evidence about galaxies

Help your learner

In this unit, learners will practise testing predictions, drawing line graphs and interpreting data (Sections 6.4 and 6.5). Section 6.5 introduces the effect that the Earth revolving has on the seasons, usually first taught at secondary level. They will also learn how scientists combine evidence with creative thinking to suggest new ideas and explanations for phenomena (Sections 6.6. and 6.7). To help them:

1 Encourage learners to find out about and follow the latest discoveries in astronomy, using the internet and news articles.

Analyse information about sunrise and sunset times

1 **a** What are **sunrise** and **sunset**?

Sunrise is _____

Sunset is _____

b What causes sunrise and sunset?

_____

Look at these two sets of sunrise and sunset times for Kuwait City, for the months of July and November.

July

Date	Sunrise time	Sunset time	Length of day
1	04:52	18:52	14 h
8	04:55	18:51	
15	04:58	18:49	
22	05:02	18:46	
29	05:06	18:43	

November

Date	Sunrise time	Sunset time	Length of day
1	06:01	17:02	
8	06:06	16:57	
15	06:11	16:53	
22	06:17	16:51	
29	06:23	16:49	

2 Fill in the length of day on both tables. The first one has been done as an example.

3 **a** Identify the pattern for the length of days in July.

_____

b What season is it in Kuwait City in July?

_____

c What season is it moving towards by the end of July? Explain your answer.

_____

_____

4 **a** Identify the pattern for the length of days in November.

_____

b What season is it in Kuwait City in November?

_____

5 Predict how the length of day will change in Kuwait City for the first three weeks of December. Explain your answer.

_____

_____

6 Draw a line graph to show the length of day in Kuwait City in November.

Remember:

Work out the scale you will use for the *y*-axis on your line graph by looking at the range of figures you have to show.

CHECK YOUR LEARNING

○ I can analyse patterns in sunrise and sunset data.

○ I can make predictions based on my scientific knowledge.

○ I can draw a line graph.

The Earth revolves around the Sun

Find information about the Earth's revolution and the seasons

Look at the diagram of Earth orbiting the Sun.

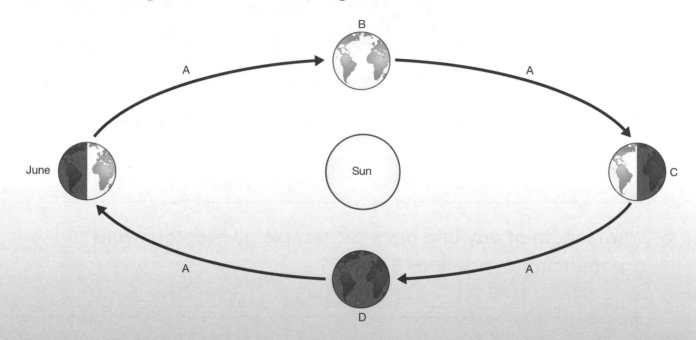

1 a Name the **orbit** labelled A.

_____

b What length of time does Earth take to complete one orbit?

_____

2 On the diagram, one of Earth's positions is labelled June. Which months do positions B, C, and D represent?

B is _____

C is _____

D is _____

3 a In the northern **hemisphere**, which season are people experiencing at position C?

_____

b What feature of the diagram tells you this?

_____

_____

4 a Which season are people all over the world experiencing at positions B and D?

_____

b What length of day and night are people all over the world experiencing at positions B and D?

_____

5 Think about it!

For how many days of the year will the Earth occupy the positions shown on the diagram? Explain your answer.

_____

_____

_____

CHECK YOUR LEARNING

◯ I can interpret a diagram of the Earth's **revolution** around the Sun.

◯ I can predict what is happening at different times of the year.

6.6 Exploring the solar system

Explore comets

Read the information about comets and answer questions using your scientific knowledge of the solar system.

Most comets are so small and so far away that we cannot see them, even using the biggest telescopes. But we can see them when they head inwards towards the Sun. The heat of the Sun makes the ice turn into gas, which streams for millions of kilometres from the **nucleus** of the comet into space.

1 **A long time ago, people called comets 'hairy stars'. Why do you think they were called this?**

_____

2 **Draw what you think a comet looks like when it moves towards the Sun.**

Rosetta was the first spacecraft sent to a comet. It was launched in 2004 and arrived at Comet 67P/Churyumov-Gerasimenko ten years later. Since then, it has been sending details about the comet back to scientists on Earth.

The comet takes 6.5 years to orbit the Sun and was closest to the Sun in August 2015. After that, the comet began to move further away. Soon there will not be enough solar power to run *Rosetta*'s scientific instruments. Scientists will note how the comet's activity decreases as it moves away from the Sun and compare this data with the data they got when the comet was approaching the Sun. There are also plans for *Rosetta* to fly across the night-side of the comet to collect dust samples **ejected** close to the nucleus. Scientists hope to end the mission by landing *Rosetta* on the comet.

3 **Why did it take ten years for *Rosetta* to reach the comet?**

_____

_____

4 **Why will *Rosetta*'s scientific instruments run out of power?**

_____

_____

5 **What is the 'night-side' of the comet?**

_____

Remember:

All bodies in the solar system move in orbits around the Sun.

6 Think about it!

Do you think people will ever be able to land on a comet?
Why or why not?

_____

_____

_____

_____

_____

CHECK YOUR LEARNING

○ I can see that ideas about comets changed as new evidence was found.

○ I can use my scientific knowledge about the solar system to help me to understand a case study.

universe, galaxy, astronomers, telescope

Finding galaxies in space

1 a Rate the following from smallest to largest: star, **universe**, **galaxy**.

_____

b In which galaxy is our solar system?

_____

Read about how astronomers find galaxies in space, then answer the questions.

The Hubble **telescope** is the best instrument available for galaxy counting and estimation. It was first launched in 1990. In 1995, astronomers pointed the Hubble telescope at what looked like an empty part of space, but they observed around 3000 faint galaxies in a single image. They called this image the Hubble Deep Field. It was the furthest anyone had seen into the universe at the time.

Scientists continued to improve the Hubble telescope. Astronomers repeated the experiment twice. In 2003 and 2004, scientists created the Hubble Ultra Deep Field, which revealed about 10,000 galaxies.

In 2012, again using upgraded instruments, scientists used the telescope to look at a portion of the Ultra Deep Field. Even in this narrower field of view, astronomers detected an extra 5500 galaxies. Researchers called this the eXtreme Deep Field.

So far Hubble has revealed an estimated 100 billion galaxies in the universe. This will probably increase to about 200 billion as telescope technology in space improves.

2 Complete the following table of research done by astronomers using the Hubble telescope.

Date	Image	Number of galaxies
	Hubble Deep Field	
2003–04		
		5500 in the same image of Hubble Ultra Deep Field

3 Why have astronomers managed to see more and more galaxies over the years?

_____

The universe is expanding faster than the speed of light. It is also accelerating (getting quicker) in its expansion. So, as the universe gets older and bigger, galaxies move further away from Earth. Astronomers measure how fast galaxies are moving away from us as the universe expands. This has helped them work out that the universe is about 13.82 billion years old.

4 What method have astronomers used to work out the age of the universe?

_____

_____

CHECK YOUR LEARNING

◯   I understand that our knowledge of the universe increases as telescopes become more and more powerful.

◯   I can use my scientific knowledge about the universe to help me understand a case study.

Answers

1 Investigating plant growth

1.3

Complete a report about germination

1 Aim: I am going to investigate if seeds need <u>light</u> to germinate.

Factors I will keep the same are:
<u>the type of seed</u>
<u>the plant pot and soil used</u>
<u>the amount of water each pot gets</u>
I will change <u>the amount of light each pot gets</u>.
I will measure <u>the number of seeds that germinate after a certain time.</u>
My prediction is that the seeds in <u>both pots</u> will germinate <u>at the same rate</u>.
My conclusion is that seeds <u>do not need light</u> for germination.

2 To make sure that that at least some seeds germinated; to be sure that she did not make a mistake in her findings.

3 No. She only did the investigation twice with three seeds. Kumei should use more seeds and repeat the investigation a few more times.

4 Repeat the investigation using lots of different kinds of seed.

5 **Think about it!**
Plants that need smoke for germination include some ericas and proteas from South Africa, the purple coneflower and sagebrush from North America, and acacias, eucalyptus and the desert raisin bush from Australia.

1.4

Grow a plant from a cutting

1 The jar should be left in a warm, sunny place.

2 The roots.

3 Learners should measure the length of the new roots and record their own data in the table.

4 Learners should draw a line graph of their own data.

1.5

Investigate plant growth

1

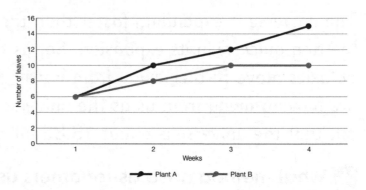

2 Plant A grew better. The evidence shows that Plant A grew more leaves than Plant B.

3 The drawing should show two leaves – Plant A as a green, healthy-looking leaf; the Plant B leaf should be very pale yellow or white and be smaller.

4 Light.

2 The life cycle of flowering plants

2.2

Identify ways that animals disperse seeds

1

Seed	Animal that disperses the seed	Way the seed is dispersed
cherry	birds, person or any other fruit-eating animal	The animal eats the fruit and the seeds pass through the animal's body and are spread in its droppings. Humans throw away the seeds.
devil's claw	sheep, goat, person or any animal with fur or wool	The seed sticks to the animal's fur or person's clothes.
sunflower	mouse, squirrel, ant	The animal buries the seeds.

2 The fruit is brightly coloured and fleshy with a nice taste.

3 The seed has hooks or spines to catch onto the animal's fur or person's clothes.

2.3

Analyse the results of an experiment with seeds

1 a

Type of seed	Time in the air 1	Time in the air 2	Time in the air 3	Average time in the air
one-winged sycamore seed	9 seconds	10 seconds	11 seconds	10 seconds
dandelion parachute	20 seconds	22 seconds	24 seconds	22 seconds
two-winged helicopter tree seed	15 seconds	13 seconds	17 seconds	15 seconds

b

Type of seed	Distance travelled 1	Distance travelled 2	Distance travelled 3	Average distance travelled
one-winged sycamore	1.8 m	2.0 m	2.2 m	2.0 m
dandelion parachute	4.5 m	4.1 m	4.3 m	4.3 m
two-winged helicopter tree seed	2.0 m	2.4 m	2.2 m	2.2 m

2 To make their results more reliable.

3 The longer the seed stays in the air, the further it travels. The dandelion seed is the lightest so it stays longest in the air and therefore can travel further. The number of wings on the seed could affect how long it stays in the air and how far it travels.

4 a Height from which seed is dropped and type of seed.

   b Speed of fan and type of seed.

5 They kept the following factors the same: height from which the seeds were dropped, distance the seed was held away from the fan and the speed of the fan.

2.4

Label the parts of a flower

1 A = anther; B = ovary; C = stigma; D = sepal.

2 The petals.

3 a Yellow, orange or brown. The anther contains the pollen, which is yellow/orange/brown.

   b Green. It is a sepal, which a small green leaf on the outside of the flower.

4 There are three sepals and three stamens.

2.6

Find out about the cannonball tree

1 The fruits are large, round and heavy, like cannonballs.

2 **a** The colour and scent of the flowers attract insects.

    b Bats are attracted by the scent of the flowers. They have very poor eyesight and visit the flowers at night when there is no light, so they cannot see the colour of the flowers.

    c They carry pollen to other flowers and pollinate them.

3 **a** The fruit falls to the ground and breaks open. The smell of the fruit attracts animals that eat the fruit.

    b The animals eat the fruit, which contains the seeds. The seeds pass through the animals' bodies and are spread in their droppings.

    c The tree can form 1000 fruits. Each fruit forms from the ovary of a flower, so if there are 1000 flowers there could be 1000 fruits.

4 **Think about it!**

The cannonball tree grows in many countries in Asia, including Thailand, Malaysia and Indonesia. It also grows in the in the Caribbean, Hawaii and the northern parts of South America – where it originated.

2.7

Describe the life cycle of plants

1 **c** germination → growth → pollination → fertilisation → seed production → seed dispersal.

2 **b** before pollination.

3 **c** the pollen joins with the egg in the ovary.

4 **d** Flowers release seeds.

5 **a** seeds form.

3 States of matter

3.3

Experiment with evaporation

1

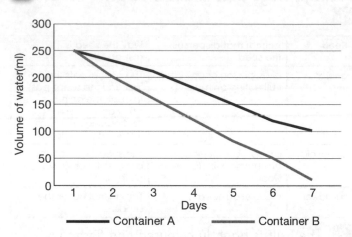

2 **a** Container B. There was less water left in the container at the end of the investigation.

    b The size of the open surface of the container.

    c Evaporation happens when water particles turn to water vapour and escape from the surface of the liquid. The bigger the surface, the more quickly the particles can escape, so evaporation happens faster.

3 Possible measurements for Days 6 and 7 are:

Container	Day 6	Day 7
A	120ml	100ml
B	50ml	10ml

3.4

Making solutions

1 a, b and c

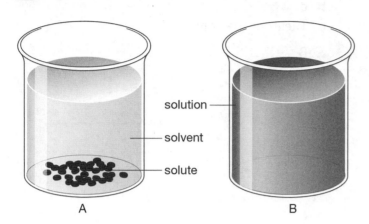

solution

solvent

solute

A   B

2 The solute (coffee powder) dissolved in the solvent (water). The particles of coffee powder moved in between the particles of water so they cannot be seen in the solution.

3 Leave the solution in a warm place so the liquid will evaporate.

3.7

Compare temperatures at which liquids boil

1 Boiling point.

2 a Cooking oil.
   b Nail polish remover.
   c 130°C.

3 a The particles of the liquid gain energy and change into a gas.
   b Evaporation.
   c

	Name of process: boiling	Name of process: evaporation
Is the process fast or slow?	fast	slow
Do bubbles form?	yes	no
At what temperature does it take place	only at higher temperatures	at room temperature
Does it happen at the surface or throughout the liquid?	throughout the liquid	at the surface
Where does the energy needed for the process come from?	from a heat source	from the environment

4 **Think about it!**
Cooking oil boils at a much higher temperature than water. So if you burn yourself with hot oil, the burn will be worse than a burn from hot water.

3.8

Compare the melting points of solids

1

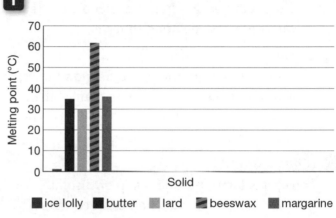

■ ice lolly ■ butter ▨ lard ▨ beeswax ▨ margarine

2 a Beeswax.
   b Ice lolly.

3 a The solids that contain fats melt at a higher temperature than the solid that is made mainly of water.
   b No. You would have to test the melting points of a number of other solids that contain a lot of fat or a lot of water and compare their melting points.

4 Butter and margarine will melt at room temperature in very warm places, so they should be kept in the fridge so they stay solid.

4 The way we see things

4.1

Explain how we see objects

1 The fire and the Moon.

2 **a** The wood and the Moon.
  b Draw a line from the Moon to the wood, with an arrow pointing to the wood, then draw another line from the wood to his eyes, with an arrow pointing to his eyes.

3 **a** The fire.
  b Draw a line from the fire to Sergio's father, with an arrow pointing to his father, then another line from his father to Sergio's eyes, with arrow pointing to his eyes.

4 **Think about it!**
Torch, gas lamp, paraffin lamp or a solar-powered lamp that they had charged during the day when the Sun was shining.

4.2

Use mirrors to see in front of and behind you

1 An image of yourself.

2 **a** With your back to the mirror on the wall.
  b In front and to one side of you.

3

4.5

Show how light is reflected

1 **a** Rays.
  b d.
  c They are the same.

2 **a** B.
  b

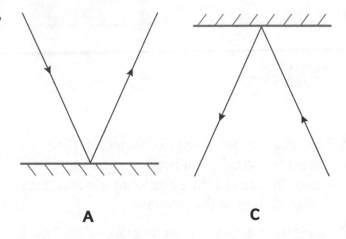

A   C

5 Shadows

5.1

Investigate the way light travels

1

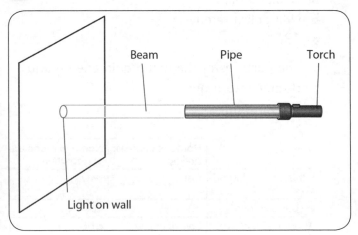

2

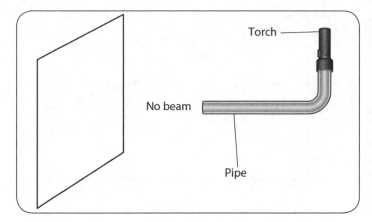

5.5

Observe how shadows change at different times of day

1 **a** In front of the bench.
b Behind them, on the other side of the palm tree.

2 Because the Sun is overhead.

3 As the Sun is lower in the sky, the shadow becomes longer.

4

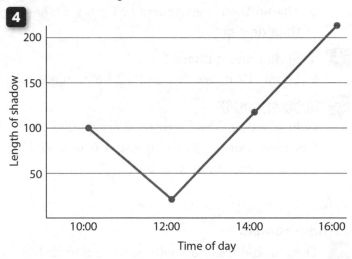

5.6

Find out how distance affects light intensity

1 Learners carry out the experiment and record their measurements in the table.

2 The further the torch is from the wall, the more squares on the paper will be lit up.

3 Learners carry out the experiment and record the measurements in the table.

4 Low light intensity.

5 The <u>greater</u> the distance, the lower the light intensity.

5.7

Measuring the speed of light

1 A rotating toothed wheel, a mirror, a light.

2 A stopwatch.

3 A rotating mirror, a fixed mirror, a light, an instrument to measure angles.

4 The angles at which light is reflected off the mirrors.

5

Date	Scientist	Speed of light
1849	Louis Fizeau	313,300 km/s
1862	Leon Foucault	299,796 km/s
Today		299,792.458 km/s

6 **Think about it!**
Galileo used two lamps at a certain distance apart to measure the speed of light. He concluded that light travels at least ten times faster than the speed of sound.

6 Earth's movements

6.4

Analyse information about sunrise and sunset times

1 **a** Sunrise is the time when the Sun appears to rise over the horizon.
Sunset is the time when the Sun appears to sink below the horizon.

b The rotation of the Earth on its axis.

2 July

Date	Sunrise time	Sunset time	Length of day
1	04:52	18:52	14 h
8	04:55	18:51	13 h 56 m
15	04:58	18:49	13 h 51 m
22	05:02	18:46	13 h 48 m
29	05:06	18:43	13 h 37 m

November

Date	Sunrise time	Sunset time	Length of day
1	06:01	17:02	11 h 01 m
8	06:06	16:57	10 h 51 m
15	06:11	16:53	10 h 42 m
22	06:17	16:51	10 h 34 m
29	06:23	16:49	10 h 26 m

3 **a** The days are getting shorter.

b Summer.

c Autumn – if the days are getting shorter, they must be moving towards the next season, which is autumn.

4 **a** The days are getting shorter.

b Winter.

5 The days will get shorter. It is moving towards the middle of winter in December.

6

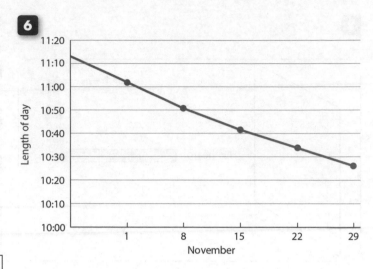

6.5

Find information about the Earth's revolution and the seasons

1 **a** Revolution.

b 365¼ days.

2 B is September.
C is December.
D is March.

3 **a** Winter.

b The northern hemisphere has more darkness than daylight.

4 **a** Spring and autumn.

b Equal: 12 hours day and 12 hours night.

5 **Think about it!**
Only one day. The Earth revolves around the Sun continuously, so every day it is in a slightly different position in its orbit.

6.6

Explore comets

1 They looked like stars with shining hair drifting behind them. The shining hair was the comet's tail.

2

3 Because the comet is on the edge of the solar system, a very long way from Earth.

4 Because they run on solar power. Once the comet moves too far away from the Sun, there will not be enough solar power.

5 The side facing away from the Sun.

6 **Think about it!**
No. It is too far – it would take ten years even to get there. When the comet moves towards the Sun you would burn to death and when the comet moves away from the Sun you would freeze to death. There is no oxygen.

6.7

Finding galaxies in space

1 **a** Star, galaxy, universe.
 b The Milky Way.

2

Date	Image	Number of galaxies
1995	Hubble Deep field	3000
2003–04	Hubble Ultra Deep Field	10,000
2012	Hubble eXtreme Deep Field	5500 in the same image of Hubble Ultra Deep Field

3 The technology of the Hubble telescope continued to improve.

4 They measure how fast galaxies are moving away from us.

 # Glossary

1 Investigating plant growth

cutting	part of a plant, such as leaves or stems, that can grow into a new plant
evidence	information gained from an experiment or investigation
factors	things that have an effect on other things
germinate	when a seed starts to grow
seeds	the parts of a plant that can grow into a new plant

2 The life cycle of flowering plants

average	the amount you get when you add together several quantities and divide the total by the number of quantities you added
dispersed	spread over a wide area
embryo	the tiny plant inside a seed that can grow into a new plant
fertilisation	the process that joins the pollen and eggs to make seeds
germination	when a seed starts to grow
life cycle	the different stages in a plant's life from when it grows from a seed to when it makes its own seeds
pollen	a yellow or brown powder made in the stamen
pollination	the process that brings pollen from the stamen to the stigma of a flower
pollinators	living or non-living things that carry pollen from the anthers to the stigma of a flower
sepals	the outer ring of small green leaves on the base of a flower
wind-dispersed	seeds or fruits that are spread by the action of wind

3 States of matter

boil	when a liquid changes to a gas at a high temperature
evaporation	when a liquid turns to a gas
factor	things that have an effect on other things
melt	when a solid changes to a liquid
melting point	the temperature at which a solid melts
solute	the substance or material that dissolves
solution	a mixture made from a solute dissolved in a solvent
solvent	the liquid in which the solute dissolves
temperature	a measurement of how hot or cold something is

4 The way we see things

angle	the number of degrees between a horizontal and a line
beams	bands that light travels in
depict	show in a certain way
light source	a place where light comes from, for example the Sun or a torch
mirror	a very smooth, shiny surface that reflects light well
object	the thing that is reflected
rays	beams of light
reflect	bounce off a surface
surfaces	the top layer that is next to air

5 Shadows

beam	a band that light travels in
conclusion	the decision you come to when you have all the evidence
evidence	information gained from an experiment or investigation
light intensity	a measure of the amount of light in an area
rotating	spinning round and round
shadow	formed when light is blocked by some types of solid object

6 Earth's movements

astronomers	scientists who study the universe
comets	lumps of ice and dirt that move in large orbits around the Sun
ejected	thrown out
galaxy	a huge mass of stars grouped together
hemisphere	half the Earth, for example the northern hemisphere is between the equator and the North Pole
nucleus	the central core of a comet
orbit	the path taken when a body moves around a larger body in space
revolution	the movement of a planet around the Sun in an orbit, or any other body in the universe moving around a bigger body
solar system	the Sun, with eight planets and other bodies such as dwarf planets, moons and asteroids revolving around it
sunrise	the time when the Sun appears to rise over the horizon
sunset	the time when the Sun appears to sink below the horizon
telescope	an instrument with magnifying mirrors for studying the stars and other bodies in space
universe	the whole of space

Remember:

Use these words when you discuss the topics in the unit so that learners become familiar with them.